The Day The Sky Fell

A Split Second That Changed Everything

Lucie Gabrielová DeLaney

de'luga Publishing

This is a work of creative nonfiction based on true events.
All names and events are presented as they occurred,
with the consent of those mentioned.
The story is portrayed to the best of the author's memory
and perspective.

Some childhood letters, drawings, and signatures appear
throughout this book. They are shared with affection
and gratitude, preserved as they were originally written,
in the spirit of honoring those who were part of the journey.

Published by de'luga Publishing

First Edition
Printed in the United States of America

ISBN: 979-8-9986200-1-0

"Out of suffering have emerged the strongest souls,
the most massive characters are seared with scars."
— Kahlil Gibran

To the girl I once was—
the one who fell so hard,
she thought she'd never get back up.
And to anyone who's ever felt like her.
This is for you.
You are not broken.
You are becoming.

For the ones who stood by me
when I couldn't stand at all.
For every friend who wrote,
called, prayed, or waited.
For the child who lost everything—
and still chose to believe in tomorrow.

To my parents—
who carried me when
I could no longer move,
who stayed when others couldn't,
who never once looked at me
like I was less.
You gave me breath when
I couldn't find my own.
You gave me everything.
Your love built the light I walk in now.
This book is part of you.

Words from the Court

Ahoj Lucko,
pamatuju si, jak jsme se těšili na ty výjezdy —
bylo to jako náš tábor. Tolik srandy na cestách,
při turnajích. Narovinu, ani si moc nepamatuju,
jak jsme hráli, ale ten pocit, že to byly krásné chvíle,
ten ve mně zůstal.

A pak přišla ta špatná zpráva. Šok.
Člověk si vůbec neuvědomuje,
že se něco takového může stát. Ani nevím,
kdo mi to tehdy řekl, ale bylo to hrozně smutné.

Ale jak se říká, každá mince má dvě strany —
a ty jsi ukázala tu svou. Ukázala jsi,
jaká jsi bojovnice. Dokázala jsi to zvrátit,
dostat se z toho a dneska máš fajn život. I po tom všem.

Myslím, že právě ta tenisová disciplína,
kterou sis nesla od dětství, ti hodně pomohla.

— Tomáš Berdych
Bývalá světová čtyřka ve dvouhře
Finalista Wimbledonu
Dvojnásobný vítěz Davis Cupu

I remember those early days when we were different.
When other kids were doing ordinary things,
we were packing for tournaments.
Those trips were our version of summer camp.
I don't even remember the matches we played.
But I remember how much fun we had.
How we looked forward to being on the road.
How much we laughed.

And then... the shock. The day I heard what had
happened to you. I don't even remember who told me.
Just that it felt unreal. Impossible. Sad beyond words.

But you—you showed the other side of the coin.
You showed what kind of fighter you are.
You turned something unimaginable
into a new kind of life. A good one.

And I truly believe that your tennis discipline,
that mindset you had from a young age—
helped you find your way through it all.

— Tomáš Berdych
Former World No. 4 in Singles
Wimbledon Finalist
Two-Time Davis Cup Champion

Pamatuju si, že když jsme byly malé, patřila jsi mezi
velké talenty a hrála jsi velmi průbojný tenis.
Byla jsi o rok starší — ročník 85, já 86 —
a vím, že v tobě lidé viděli velké naděje.
Patřila jsi k největším talentům českého tenisu.
A proto jsi trénovala na Štvanici a pak se najednou
roznesla zpráva, že se ti stalo velké zranění páteře.
Udělala jsi špatný kotoul při kondiční přípravě
a najednou jsi ležela v nemocnici. Nemohla ses hýbat.

Všichni se ptali, co se vlastně stalo, kdo za to může,
co s tebou bude. Nikdo nechápal, jak se to mohlo
při kondičním tréninku stát.
A od té doby jsme se my, holky, hrozně bály dělat
jakékoli gymnastické prvky.
Pamatuju si, že jsme mezi sebou řešily,
kdo tě může jít navštívit. Vím, že za tebou chodila
Verča Kuchařová a vždycky nám o tobě něco řekla.
Tak jsme měli aspoň nějaké zprávy.
A všichni jsme drželi palce, že budeš bojovat.

Ale v té době nepřevládala moc naděje,
že to dobře dopadne. A pak jsme tě viděly. Stála jsi,
mohla jsi chodit, mluvila jsi s námi.
Měly jsme obrovskou radost.
Ale taky jsme si všechny uvědomily, jak tenká
je ta hranice mezi tím, že to dobře dopadlo, a tím,
že to mohlo dopadnout ještě hůř.

Tvůj příběh jsem pak vnímala znovu,
když jsem tě potkala na turnaji v Cincinnati.
Dostala se ke mně knížka tvé maminky,
kde popisuje, čím jste si obě prošly.
Tehdy jsem teprve začala chápat, kolik bolesti
za tím vším bylo. Člověk si neuvědomí, že nejde
jen o psychickou zátěž nebo omezení.
Ale o obrovskou bolest — fyzickou i duševní.

Jsem ráda, že tě dnes vidím šťastnou, spokojenou,
s krásnou rodinou a zdravými dětmi.
Držím ti palce, ať tě život zavede kamkoli.
Měj se hezky. Pusu, Andrejka

— **Andrea Sestini Hlaváčková**
Bývalá 3. hráčka světa ve čtyřhře
Trojnásobná grandslamová vítězka
Olympijská medailistka a vítězka Fed Cupu

I remember when we were little you stood out as
a bold, fearless tennis player.
You were one year older — born in '85, I'm from '86 —
and I remember how people saw you as a great hope.
You were one of the brightest talents in Czech tennis.
That's why you trained at Štvanice.
And then suddenly, the news broke.

You had done a somersault during fitness training
and something went terribly wrong.
You were in the hospital. You couldn't move.

Everyone was asking what happened.
Who was responsible? What now?
No one could understand how such a thing
could happen during a fitness training.
And from then on, we girls were terrified
to try any kind of gymnastics.

I remember how we whispered
about who would go visit you.
Veronika Kuchařová would go see you
and bring us little updates.
That's how we knew you were fighting.
And we were all rooting for you.

But back then, there wasn't much hope.
And then we saw you again.
You stood. You walked. You spoke with us.
And we were filled with joy.

But at the same time, we realized how thin
the line is between a good ending and a terrible one.

Later, I heard your story again when we met
at the tournament in Cincinnati.
I got your mom's book, and for the first time,
I understood the full weight of what you went through.

Until then, I hadn't realized how much physical
pain had accompanied it all.
It's not just about limits, or mental endurance,
or lost potential. It's about real pain in the body
and in the soul.

I'm so happy to see you today happy,
fulfilled, surrounded by a beautiful family
and healthy children.

I wish you all the best wherever life leads you next.
With love,
Andrejka

— Andrea Sestini Hlaváčková
Former World No. 3 in Doubles
Three-Time Grand Slam Champion
Olympic Medalist & Fed Cup Winner

Pamatuju si Tě jako sebevědomou,
bezstarostnou, nadějnou sportovkyni.
Tenistku plnou energie.
A pak jako holku, která najednou — příliš brzy —
zjistí, co je život.

Hrozně jsem Tě obdivoval.

— Martin Pazdera

Pan učitel tělesné výchovy
Trenér sportovní gymnastiky

I remember you as a confident, carefree,
and promising young athlete.
A tennis player full of energy.
And then—a girl who suddenly, far too early,
came to understand what life really is.

I admired you deeply.

— Martin Pazdera

PE Teacher
Gymnastics Coach

My first high level doubles tournament
where I was able to play together
with a top player (you) and we placed 3rd.
It really sparked my joy in playing doubles!
We beat some great teams there!

— Olga Shaw (née Klímová)

Author's Note

It took me twenty-five years to understand what
really happened to me.
Not just physically—but spiritually. Silently.
Deep in the parts of me that no doctor could scan
and no medicine could reach.

For a long time, I thought what happened
was a punishment. A mistake.
Something to be endured and buried.
But time, healing, and truth showed me
there was more.

This wasn't punishment.
It was awakening.

It took twenty-five years to finally understand that
this wasn't the end of my story.
It was the beginning of my purpose.

I was meant to speak up.
I was meant to write this.
To heal not just myself, but to offer
that healing to others.
To show what it looks like when life shatters...
and the soul decides to rise anyway.

This isn't just a memoir about paralysis or pain.
It's about rediscovery. Resilience.
And how the deepest scars often hold
the most sacred light.

If you are holding this book, I want you to know:
You don't have to be fearless to begin.
You just have to be honest.
This story found me for a reason.
And now, it's found you too.
It's a mirror held out for anyone
who needs to see their own strength again.

You're not broken.
You're becoming.
And I'm right here with you.

With love and purpose,
Lucie

Opening Page

I didn't plan on becoming
a story people remembered.
At fourteen, I only wanted to disappear.
I wanted to go back—to the moment
before the stillness, before the doctors,
before the ceiling tiles became my sky.

But life had other plans.
Not to punish me.
To awaken me.

This isn't just a story about survival.
It's the "let me show you what light is born
through fire" kind of story.

Because what broke me open didn't end me.
It rebuilt me.

My injury didn't define me.
It refind me.
It led me deeper—
into truth, into healing,
into a life where silence became voice,
stillness became presence,
and pain became purpose.

This is not just my story.
It's a mirror—for anyone
who's ever felt broken,
forgotten, or stuck in a life
they didn't ask for.

You're not broken either.
You're becoming.

Prologue

Before the Fall

There was a time when my body felt like home.
When my legs answered without question.
When breath moved freely and
I never once wondered what it meant to be able.

I didn't know the sky could fall.
Not yet.

I knew only movement—
footsteps pounding red clay,
the swing of a racquet,
a heart full of fire and forward motion.

I was fourteen,
and the world was still a promise.

I had no idea that one day,
the simple act of standing would become a miracle.
That silence would scream louder than pain.
That I would wake up in a body I couldn't feel
and have to learn how to live inside the stillness.

But the soul remembers what the mind cannot.
Even in those early days—
when I ran without fear,
when I built dreams on courts my dad swept clean,
a knowing followed me.

That life wouldn't go as planned.
But it would go exactly as it must.

This is not a story about being broken.
It's a story about becoming.
And this—this last breath
before everything changed—
is where it begins.

The Spark

My dad wasn't a tennis player.

But both of my parents wanted a better life—
for me and for my brother.
So when the tides of change swept across our country,
when the grip of communism loosened and
freedom peeked through—the chance to dream
screamed out loud.

With bare hands and devoted hope,
they built tennis courts.
Clay, wire, sweat, and belief—
rooted into the earth like a promise.
In a tucked-away corner of our town, behind houses
and hedges, a place was born.

I was six, maybe seven, the day I found it:
A small wooden racquet with a red handle.
Forgotten in the corner. Weathered. Waiting.

I'd swing it wildly at the green hitting wall,
chasing the bounce, trying again and again.
I didn't know the rules. I didn't need to.
I only knew it felt like magic.

That wooden racquet became my first real friend.
The green wall, my first opponent.
And the rhythm—the bounce, the breath, the swing—
became my heartbeat.

One day, as I played alone
with all the focus my little body could hold,
one of my dad's friends stopped to watch.
After a few moments,
he turned to my dad and said:

"She's actually pretty good.
You want to do something about that?"

That was it.
A spark.

From that point on, tennis wasn't just something I did.
It was something that lived in me.

Cathedrals of Clay and Sky

In a hidden corner of Prague, where the scent of
blooming flowers mingled with the warm breath of
morning, there sat a humble set of tennis courts—
cradled between rows of sleepy homes and stories
waiting to be lived.

To most, they were just cracked clay and faded
white lines. But to me? They were everything.
This was my cathedral. My escape.
My proving ground.

From sunrise to sunset, I lived there—
barefoot sometimes, wild-haired, driven and radiant.
The world beyond the fences didn't matter
when I was on those courts. I wasn't just playing tennis.
I was becoming someone.

To passersby, I might've seemed intense. Obsessed.
But I wasn't chasing medals.
I was chasing freedom.

Because out there—on that red clay—
I wasn't just a girl.
I was fire. I was flight. I was limitless.

No one could've known then how much those courts
would come to mean.
Or how long I would carry the memory of them...
once I could no longer walk across them.

The yellow building watched over the courts.
Inside were the modest locker rooms, a cozy
reception desk, and the warm presence of my mom—
always there, always watching,
holding everything together with grace.
She wasn't just working.
She was anchoring the world I was creating.

Out back, behind the green hitting wall,
my imagination blossomed.
I wasn't just practicing my swings—
I was building realms. Every line became a
threshold to another adventure.
Every bounce of the ball echoed with possibility.
Overhead, red and pink flowers spilled like soft
confetti down the fences, planted and tended
lovingly by my dad's hands.
His constant devotion was everywhere.
In the petals, the pathways, the peace.

6

He didn't just grow flowers.
He grew beauty so I could grow dreams.

That place wasn't just a tennis club.
It was my sacred space.
A sanctuary built from love, sweat, clay, and sky.
I would carry the memory of this place through
every chapter of my life that followed.

In this enchanted world I called mine, every day
unfolded like a symphony—one of play, grit,
and pure imagination. The rhythm of my life
was a dance between determination and wonder,
between fierce practice and wild freedom.

Beyond the boundaries of the court, I was more
than an athlete. I was an adventurer. A dreamer.
A creator of worlds.

I crafted make-believe matches in my mind,
calling out scores to invisible crowds as I swung
at shadows and sunlight. I scaled fences like a girl
with wings, exploring the hidden corners
of my domain as if the entire universe lived inside
this little patch of clay and hope.

Every jump rope became a storyline.
Every ball, a spark of magic.
Every game of hide and seek—
played with companions only I could see—
filled the air with a laughter that didn't need
an echo to be remembered.

Those courts weren't just for tennis.
They were for becoming.
And every inch of that space—every flower,
every fence, every crack in the pavement—
held the fingerprints of my childhood
and the heartbeat of a girl who believed
in something bigger than herself.

This was where I felt most alive. Most free.
In this world, where the borders between fantasy
and reality softened, anything felt possible.

Here, I wasn't limited by fear or gravity or expectation.
I was bold. Boundless. Unbreakable.

But life has a way of shifting
when you least expect it.
And though I couldn't yet see
the storm on the horizon,
I would soon learn
that even the most magical places
aren't safe from pain.
That this cherished sanctuary—
my kingdom of red clay and wild dreams—
would one day become the place I'd fight to return to,
not just as a player, but as a survivor.

The Camp That Taught Me More than Tennis

The picturesque town of Jindřichův Hradec,
with its cobbled streets and centuries-old rooftops,
nestled beyond the bustle of Prague,
guarded like a secret from the rest of the world.
It was here, in this postcard-perfect setting,
that I was sent to my very first tennis camp—a place
where competition and friendship wove themselves
together in ways I never could have predicted.

I arrived unprepared.
Stepping onto the clay courts in nothing
but a pair of flip-flops, my racquet dangling
awkwardly by my side. I barely knew the rules.
I barely knew how things worked.
It wasn't long before the coach,
a kind but no-nonsense figure, corrected me sharply,
setting the tone for a week that would stretch
and shape me far beyond my expectations.

Between drills and long, sweaty afternoons
under the sun, life at camp flourished with small
adventures. Little moments that somehow
never left me, just living inside me.

One of those days is rooted in my heart
with laughter and a little pinch of shame.

I was assigned an older roommate, someone
I admired instantly for her easy confidence
and cool demeanor. One afternoon, she casually
offered me something I had never seen before:
a crinkled bag of bacon-flavored chips.
They smelled like rebellion.
They tasted like something forbidden and irresistible.

At first, I told myself I would have just one. Just one.

But the moment the salty, smoky flavor hit my tongue,
I was hooked. When my roommate left the room,
the bag whispered my name from inside the closet.
I fought the temptation... for a while. Then, as if pulled
by an invisible string, I crept over, slipped my hand
inside, and took another. And another. And another.

Before I knew it, half the bag was gone,
and I was sitting on the floor with crumbs on my shirt
and a growing pit of guilt in my stomach.
The closet door swung shut with a thud
that sounded, in my panicked mind,
like a judge's gavel. I sat frozen, dreading the moment
she would come back. When she did,
her eyes flicked immediately to the bag.
Half empty. Wide open.
She looked at me. I looked at her.
The world held its breath.
In a moment of pure, desperate creativity,
I blurted out a lie so ridiculous
it almost made me laugh through my terror.
"I think... maybe the cleaning lady took some," I said.
Feigning innocence with the clumsiest of shrugs.

Whether she believed me, or simply decided
to spare me the humiliation, I'll never know.
She didn't press.
She just smiled—a little too knowingly—
and went back to unpacking her things.

That tiny moment—half funny, half aching
with shame—taught me about temptation.
About honesty. About the secret grace of being
forgiven even when you don't quite deserve it.
To remember that friendship is often built
in the spaces where we're real, awkward,
and trying our best.

And even now, whenever I smell bacon chips,
I'm right back there—eight years old,
barefoot on a clay floor, learning in the softest,
most human way that growth isn't always
about winning or losing.
Sometimes, it's about recognizing the messy,
imperfect places where we stumble...
and choosing to keep walking forward anyway.

The First Lessons
of the Arena

When I first dipped my toes into the world
of tennis tournaments, I was just nine years old—
a soft-hearted girl who believed
that kindness would be enough to carry me
through any battle. I still remember the feeling
of walking onto the court for my very first match:
the crisp, new scent of my tennis bag,
heart pounding in my chest,
nerves buzzing like a thousand fireflies trapped
inside me. My opponent stood across the net,
a little taller, a little more confident, but to me,
she was just another child like me—a potential friend.

In my innocence, I looked at her with an open smile
and, without thinking, let the words slip out:
"You're going to win. You're better than me."
I meant it as a compliment. A gesture of humility.
But in that moment, I had unknowingly surrendered
the match before it even began.

With each rally, my naivety showed itself.
When she struck the ball out
by a wide margin, I didn't call it.
I awarded her the point without question,
wanting more to be kind than to be right.
When she hesitated, I assured her
she had played it perfectly.
My heart was full of goodwill, but my spirit
was still learning how to stand its ground.

It didn't take long for the lesson to find me.
I realized, slowly and painfully, that the kindness
I so freely gave would not always be returned.
The court was not just a playground.
It was a battlefield.

There, beneath the open sky and the watching eyes
of parents and coaches, I learned that sportsmanship
was not about surrender. It was about standing tall.
It was about fighting, point by point,
for the dream inside you—even when it trembled.

I walked off that court that day with a heavy heart,
the sting of defeat weighing more than the racquet
in my hand. Yet beneath the ache, I realized:
Be kind, yes. But never shrink yourself for anyone.

In tennis—as in life—I would have to learn
the delicate dance: how to be gracious but fierce.
Humble but unbreakable. To love my opponents,
but never underestimate myself.

That first painful lesson carved into me
an early truth I would carry everywhere:
the world is not always fair.
But I can be fair to myself.
I can honor the fight inside me.

And maybe, just maybe,
that would be enough to take me anywhere
I dreamed of going.

Forged in the Fire of Competition

With every serve struck into the blue sky,
with every volley exchanged across the net,
I wasn't just learning how to win or lose.
I was gathering something far more valuable.
Piece by piece, match by match, I was uncovering
the deeper layers of what it meant
to step into an arena—not just to play,
but to stand for myself.

I quickly learned that not everyone shared
my values of fairness or kindness.
Not every handshake across the net was sincere.
Sometimes, you had to fight not just for points,
but for your own dignity.
And so, through the crucible of competition,
I began to change.

I learned to speak up when a ball landed out,
to hold my ground when calls were disputed,
and that true sportsmanship wasn't about
being silent or small.

It was about playing with heart and with honor.
About keeping the fire alive inside me
while respecting the battle across the net.

Those early tournaments—with all their
innocence, heartbreak, and triumph—etched
themselves into the foundation of who I was
becoming. They taught me lessons no trophy
could ever teach: resilience, courage, and the wisdom
to know that being kind does not mean being weak.

With every match I played, I shed a little more fear.
I built muscles not just in my legs, but in my spirit.
I began to believe—not in some fairy tale of
effortless success, but in the unbreakable truth
that strength and compassion could exist side by side.

It was never just about tennis.
It was about becoming a person who could enter
any arena, any storm,
and still stand with her head held high.

A Door Closes,
A Window Opens

The rejection from the prestigious tennis club
stung deeper than I let on. For a moment,
it felt like the world had drawn a line and left me
standing on the outside, unwelcome and unseen.

But my parents—my unwavering pillars—
refused to let that be the end of the story.

Their conviction in me burned even brighter
than my own. While I wrestled with disappointment,
they set out on a mission, scouring every lead,
every whisper of a coach who might see in me
what others had missed. They refused to believe
that a single closed door could define my future.

After countless dead ends and tentative meetings,
they finally found him.

He was sixty years old, with silver-streaked hair,
kind but calculating eyes,
and the confidence of a man who had
already walked the road to greatness.
His daughter had played professionally,
but it was the way he spoke about the game—
with reverence, with passion—that captured us.
He wasn't interested in building cookie-cutter players.
He sought to carve out something rare.
Something real.

From the first day we trained together,
I could feel the difference.

His methods were unlike anything I had known—
focusing on precision, strategy, and the deeper poetry
of the game. He didn't just teach me
how to strike a ball. He taught me how to think,
how to feel the rhythm of the court, how to shape
a match like an artist shapes a canvas.

Under his patience, and guidance, my strokes
grew sharper. My footwork quicker.
My instincts stronger.

I stopped chasing the approval of others.
I started chasing my own potential.

Each session under the hot sun,
each hour spent drilling the same shot
until it lived in my bones,
formed a new kind of hunger—
not just to win,
but to become the best version of myself.

Still, the road ahead remained steep.

Despite the leaps in my training,
the higher ranks of competition
stayed just out of reach.
I entered low-level tournaments
with hope alive in my chest, only to leave
me carrying the heavy weight of near-misses
and lessons learned the hard way.
Each loss was a mirror held up to my dreams.
Showing me just how far I still had to climb.

But deep down, I came to see this:
rejection doesn't end dreams.
It shapes them.

The Flame Born from Failure

There are moments that imprint themselves
into your soul so deeply,
you can still feel them years later.

One tournament in particular
became that moment for me.

I arrived with vision in my step,
my dreams packed tightly into my tennis bag
alongside my racquets. I had trained relentlessly,
imagined every outcome, dared to trust
this might be my breakthrough.

But dreams alone aren't enough.

Before I even had a chance to compete,
I was told the truth—blunt and unyielding.
I didn't have enough points to qualify.
Not even for the preliminary rounds.

I remember standing there, shrinking inside,
my racquet slipping slightly from my grasp.
Around me, laughter erupted—not the joyful kind,
but the sharp, stinging kind meant to wound.

"She doesn't even have enough points!"
someone sneered.
Another girl snickered, loud enough for me to hear,
"Why even show up?"

Their words wrapped around me like chains.
I lowered my head, fighting the prick of tears,
and walked through the gates feeling smaller
than I had ever felt before.

But just beyond the noise,
just past the wall of shame and disappointment,
there was my dad.

He didn't rush to fix it.
He didn't make hollow promises.
He simply looked at me with firm eyes and said:
"If you give it everything for the next year,
they won't laugh next time.
They'll remember your name."

That was the moment I decided.
Not in anger. Not in spite.
But in grounded determination.

For the next twelve months, I lived on that fire.
Every early morning practice.
Every lonely evening when others were out
having fun. Every aching muscle.
Every small victory no one else saw.
I carried my dad's words like a torch inside me.

And then, slowly at first, and then all at once,
the tide began to turn.

I started winning—small matches at first,
then bigger ones. Victory after victory.
The girl who had once been laughed off the court
was now the name everyone was watching.
By the end of the season, I wasn't just competing.
I was dominating.

I became the number one player in the city.
The same prestigious club that once shut its doors
on me now came knocking, eager to bring me
into their fold. The same girls who once murmured
behind my back now whispered something
entirely different as I walked past.

"Watch out," they said. "Here she comes."

Others glanced around and asked,
"Which one is Gabrielová?"

It wasn't revenge that filled
my chest in those moments. It was pride.
Not just for the titles or the trophies—
but for the battles no one saw.
The lonely practices.
The constant perseverance.
The promise I made to myself—and kept.

Because sometimes, the greatest victories
are not the ones won before a crowd,
but the ones earned deep within yourself.

The Discipline
Behind the Dream

While others my age were planning weekend outings
or lounging by the sea, my world moved to
a different rhythm—one of calloused hands,
early wake-ups, and dogged repetition.
Tournaments filled my weekends.
Training consumed my weekdays.
And when competitions took me across cities
or even across borders, my schoolwork followed
in a stack of pages and permission slips.

The director of our school,
kind and understanding,
approved an individual study plan.
There simply wasn't space in my days
for eight hours of sitting still
when my life demanded movement,
precision, and sweat.

But not everyone understood.

To some classmates, it might have looked like
special treatment. An escape from school.
An unfair advantage. What they didn't see were
the drills behind the scenes, the aching muscles,
the missed birthday parties, the summers we traded
for clay courts and sweat-drenched shoes.

We never complained.
Tennis was more than a sport—
it was our discipline, our world.
Maybe even our addiction.
And to us, the normal rhythm of life
wasn't something we missed.
We were chasing something bigger.
Something that made every sacrifice worth it.

The Pinnacle

I will never forget the day I was chosen to represent
the Czech Republic in the European Team
Tournament-Antwerp Diamond Tennis Trophy.

We were handed matching uniforms—each one
stamped with "Czech Republic" in bold letters.
It felt official. It felt real.
I remember tracing those words, barely able to believe
they belonged to me.

We loaded into the club van, our chests tight
with adrenaline and pride, and drove to Belgium,
a country I had only seen in maps. When we arrived,
flags from all across Europe flapped in the breeze,
each one a promise of challenge, of story.
Inside the check-in area, teams gathered like waves
before the storm, waiting to be placed in the draw.

And then—we played.

I don't know if it was the energy in the air,
the pressure, the flags, the sheer magic of it all—
I played like I had never played before.

We competed in both individual and team events.
Match after match, I held my ground,
surprising everyone—including myself.

Then came the hardest match of all:
I had to face my own teammate.

She was ranked fourth in the Czech Republic.
I was two places behind her. She had beaten me
at nearly every other tournament we'd played.
We knew each other's rhythm by heart.
But this time, the momentum was mine.

This time, she didn't stand a chance.

I won.

I made it to the semifinals,
and I brought home the bronze.

And that wasn't all.

With the very same teammate
I had defeated in singles,
we entered the doubles bracket—and we won.
Match after match, we found
an untouchable rhythm.

As a team, the Czech Republic
won the entire tournament.

The closing ceremony felt like something
from a movie. They rolled out a red carpet.
When our names were called,
the speakers erupted with
"We Are the Champions" by Queen.
I can still hear it. I can still feel it.

People stood.
Cheered.
Little kids asked us for autographs—
on tennis balls, on caps,
on anything they could hand us.

And in that moment, everything felt right.
The early mornings.
The bruised knees.
The endless drills on courts.
It had all led here.

I was a champion.
Not in a dream.
Not in make-believe.

But in Europe.
In real life.

And I was just getting started.

The Last Match

I didn't know it then.

I didn't know that this would be
the last tournament of it all.

If someone had told me that morning,
while I was tying my shoes,
I wouldn't have believed them. I felt strong. Excited.
Fourteen years old, and stepping onto the court
for something big—my first Grand Prix tournament,
open only to the country's top-ranked players.

We were playing for prize money.
Money!
At fourteen.
It felt so official.
So cool.

The first round passed like a breeze.

In the second, I faced a girl I knew well.
I don't remember our stats, but I knew
stats didn't matter—not really.
In tennis, you can have a bad day,
or your opponent can simply have a better one.

I was already warming up when she arrived,
carrying a bucket of balls.

Laughing, I teased, "What's with the bucket?"
She grinned back, "It's for you—
since you'll be hitting outs all match."

Guess who ended up hitting all the outs?

She did.

Quarterfinals came next—and with it,
a new kind of pressure.

My opponent was beautiful—long blond hair,
stylish skirt, the picture-perfect teenage player.
I, on the other hand, had short hair,
usually wore shorts, and didn't really fit
that polished mold.

The court we were assigned was
right in front of the hotel.

And that's when the hockey team
from Germany showed up.

Boys. A whole team of them.
They spilled out of the hotel and gathered along
the sidelines to watch us play.
Naturally, they began cheering for her.

And I don't blame them.

Point by point, I started shifting the match in my favor.
And slowly, everything began to lean my way.

Their cheers became quieter for her.
Louder for me.
Then they were clapping just for me.

They followed me to my next match.
And the next.
High fives. Cheers. Smiles.
I didn't even care if they were cute. I just loved
that they believed in me.

They became my team.

Before the final, they had to leave.
We said goodbye like friends parting
at the edge of a summer dream—
quick hugs, good lucks passed between
young hearts that knew how to celebrate a moment.

Then came the final match.

And it was poetic.

I was playing her—my teammate
from the European tournament.
The same girl I had beaten in Belgium.
We had history.
We had heat.

It was a beautiful match—tight, focused, fierce.
I was ahead.

And then, it happened.

A nosebleed.
Sudden.
Sharp.

We had to pause.
And in that stillness, I lost it.
My rhythm.
My fire.
She seized the moment.

She played brilliantly—and in the end, she won.

I was disappointed. But not crushed.

Because that tournament gave me something bigger
than a trophy.

It gave me a taste of joy, of camaraderie, of being seen.

It gave me the thrill of rising—
and my first interview with a local paper,
where I probably stumbled over every answer
but beamed like I'd just won Wimbledon.

It gave me a moment I'd carry for the rest of my life—
even when I could no longer hold a racquet.

I didn't know it was the last match.
But I'm glad I played it like it wasn't.

The Winter of Preparation

As I neared my fifteenth birthday,
the rhythm of my life shifted again.

Winter, once a season for rest, snowflakes,
and holidays, had taken on a new meaning.
It was no longer a break.
It was a forge.

With tournaments on pause, there were
no trophies to chase, no crowds to impress—
only the grueling work that true
transformation demands.

Every morning, I laced up my shoes before the city
fully woke. I spent hours at the club,
hitting ball after ball under a sky the color of ash,
refining every stroke until my muscles knew them
better than my mind.
No shortcuts.
No applause.
Only the silent, sacred rhythm of repetition.

After practice, I headed straight to the gym.
Lifting. Sprinting. Sweating through layers.
Some days, the cold air bit into my jacket
as I stepped outside, breath rising in soft clouds,
muscles aching, legs like jelly.

The soreness was real,
but so was the change it chiseled into me.

It wasn't just strength.
It was conviction.

Every rep. Every early morning. Every unseen
choice to rise instead of rest—
it was all a promise to the girl I used to be.
The one who once left tournaments
with her head bowed and her dreams flickering.

I was no longer training to prove anything to anyone.
I wasn't running from fear anymore.
I was training for me.
For the girl I was becoming.
For the future I could almost touch.

And that future felt closer than ever.

Right before Christmas, my club sat me down
with news that nearly knocked the breath out of me.

They were preparing to send me to Florida,
to train at one of the most prestigious
tennis academies in the world.
Not for a camp.
Not for a few weeks.
For two years.

I would live there.
Train there.
Begin playing major international tournaments:
the Orange Bowl, Eddie Herr,
the kind of events that launched the careers
of players I had only ever watched on TV.

It was everything I'd worked for.
Everything I had dreamed of since
the first time I'd picked up a racquet.

I didn't scream.
I didn't cry.

I just sat with it, pulse racing.
Feeling the shape of my life beginning to change.

Florida.

It sounded like sunshine and possibility.
Like leaving the small courts of my childhood
behind and stepping fully into a life
that suddenly felt real.

I didn't know it then—
but this was the edge of all.
The moment before the page turns.
The inhale before the fall.

Winter held so much promise.

And I held it all in my hands.

The Day the Sky Fell

December 8, 1999

Outside, winter pressed itself against the windows,
wrapping the world in silence and frost.
But inside the school gym,
the air snapped with energy—
not just the sharp scent of sweat and varnished wood,
but the hum of effort, ambition, and adrenaline.

The outdoor courts had frozen over,
forcing us indoors. The gym echoed with the thud
of sneakers, the squeak of pivots,
the breathless rhythm of bodies in motion.
Thick ropes hung from the rafters like waiting trials.
A lone trampoline waited in the corner—
offering flight, and maybe... something else.

The blue crash mats beside it looked soft,
but anyone who's ever trained knows—
nothing about transformation is soft.

That day, our coach pushed us harder than ever.
We were no longer just training.
We were proving something.

The drill was simple:
Sprint.
Hit the trampoline.
Vault over the gym equipment.
Land and roll on the mats.
Fast.
Sharp.
Clean.

I watched the others go, adrenaline rising louder
with each turn. By the time I stepped to the line,
my breath came shallow.
I wiped my palms on my shorts.
Tightened my ponytail.

And then—I ran.

Hard.
Fast.
Every muscle firing, every thought silent.

The moment my feet hit the trampoline,
the world lifted.

For a breath, I was airborne—
not a girl, not a body,
just motion,
just light.

And in that perfect slice of sky,
I thought:

This is it.
This is what it means to be alive.
Free.
Limitless.
Unstoppable.

But then—

The world cracked.

In a blink, the landing disappeared.
No mat met me.
No roll softened the fall.

There was only silence.
And the sound of everything... stopping.

Darkness fell like a curtain.
Total. Sudden. Absolute.

I didn't scream.
I couldn't.

I heard nothing but the echo of my heartbeat—
loud and slow, like it was searching for a body
to belong to.

And in that suspended space,
between what had just been
and what would never be again,
I knew.

Before anyone spoke.
Before anyone reached me.
I knew.

The sky had fallen.

And nothing...
not even time
would ever be the same.

When the World Tilted

Slowly, the world seeped back into view—
a blur of shapes and worried faces hovering above me.

I lay frozen on the soft blue mat,
my body withdrawn and unfamiliar.
The ceiling lights buzzed overhead—
too bright, too far.
I couldn't move.
I couldn't feel.

My gaze drifted down to a pair of hands.

They moved slowly.
Awkwardly.
Unnaturally.

They were mine.
And yet... they weren't.

A panic clawed at my chest.

I tried to speak, my voice barely holding.
"Whose hands are these?" I gasped—
as though the question could unmake
what had just happened.
As though naming the fear would make it leave.

But before an answer came, the edges of the world
folded inward again.

Darkness.
Sirens.
The hum of urgency I could no longer reach.

Outside the gym, my dad waited in the cold—
probably humming along to the radio,
thinking of the drive home, dinner, tomorrow.

Until the sirens.

Until the ground dropped out from beneath him.

In an instant, he was running.
Toward the flashing lights.
Toward the unimaginable.

50

He found me crumpled, my body surrounded
by medics speaking in urgent, clipped tones.

He didn't hesitate.
He called my mom.
His voice was raw, a wound torn open.

"Come. Now."

Together they followed the ambulance
through the winding streets, headlights slicing
through the dark, tension coiling with a dread
too big to name.

At the emergency entrance, we met again.

Not with stories about practice.
Not with warm hugs or proud smiles.

With tears.

I was strapped to the gurney, barely conscious—
and the moment I saw my mom's face,
the world tilted and narrowed to her.

Her eyes.
Her breath.
The way her body reached for me before her mind
could catch up.

I tried to speak.

But all that came out was a sob.
A cry so full of guilt and helplessness,
I barely recognized it as my own.

And then, somehow, through the pain,
through the fog, the words came.

"I'm sorry, Mom."

They weren't just about the fall.
They were about everything.
About breaking the heart of the woman
who had held mine from the moment it began to beat.

Her arms surrounded me,
with strength and fear.

And she said the only thing a mom can say
when the ground gives way:

"You're here.
That's all that matters."

For a moment, in that broken stillness,
I believed her.

The Words
That Changed Everything

The world blurred again—
slipping from my grasp like a dream fading at sunrise.

I hovered somewhere between sleep and awareness,
a thin thread tethering me to this earth
as voices swirled above and around me—
too quick, too sharp, as if the air itself
had turned against me.

The medical team moved fast.
Their hands, practiced.
Their language, urgent.

Before they hooked me up to vital signs screens,
before the steady beeping and the heavy doors
of the MRI swallowed me whole,
there was a moment so small, yet it stayed in my heart.

The nurses approached gently, asking if they could
cut away the T-shirt I was wearing.
The one tangled awkwardly around the cervical collar
the ambulance doctors had fastened around my neck.

I told them no.

It wasn't just a shirt. It was my lucky tennis shirt—
the one I wore to tournaments and tough practices,
the one that always seemed to carry a little magic.
Some part of me still believed I'd need it again soon.
That next week, I'd be back on the court.
That this was only a pause, not the end.

What struck me most was that they listened.
They honored my answer, even when the easier thing
would have been to move quickly,
to cut without asking.

In a world that was already spiraling out of my control,
that small act of respect swathed around me
like a shield I didn't know I needed.

I was whisked away beneath fluorescent lights,
my body rolled like freight down the cold, sterile
hallways.

Machines beeped.
Doors opened.
Voices echoed.

Inside the MRI scanner, I lay still.
My body felt small.
Foreign.
A passenger inside itself.

I stared at the metal ceiling
while images were captured—
frames of a truth no one wanted to see.

Then the silence came.

And with it, the doctors.

Their faces were pale and grave,
as though they'd seen something they couldn't unsee.

"A spinal cord contusion," they said.
"Damage from vertebrae two to four."
"Swelling dangerously close to vertebra one."
"The area that controls breathing."

Breathing.

One wrong shift, one delayed decision—
and I might have stopped breathing altogether.

And then—

The words.

The ones no one is ever ready to hear.
The ones no child should ever hear.
The ones that will linger in the spaces
between every memory that came before.

"She's a quadriplegic."

They didn't shout it.
They didn't soften it.

They just said it—
like a fact, like a line in a medical file,
as if they hadn't just set fire to my entire future.

Somewhere in the haze, a part of me heard it.
A part of me knew.
And a part of me... broke.

I was almost fifteen.
I had been days away from Florida.
From big tournaments.
From running across courts, chasing a dream
rooted in every part of me.

And in a single, breathless moment
—a split second—
it was gone.

Not lost.
Not paused.
Gone.

The race I had been running was over.

And a new one—one I never asked for—
had just begun.

The First Battle

Even in the thick, sterile air of the hospital,
life refused to vanish.

Just after the MRI, a nurse—calm, observant,
and composed—noticed something
others had missed. A spark.
The barest tremble in my finger.
But it was enough.
Enough to say:
I'm still here.

The doctors gathered.
Faces tight. Voices low.
Surgery was an option—dangerous, invasive,
full of risk.
But instead, they chose to flood my body
with powerful corticosteroids—an aggressive attempt
to stop the swelling and hope that my spinal cord
might begin to heal on its own.

And so, without warning, the war began.

The first week bled into a nightmare of survival
—one I couldn't wake from.
Pain tore through me in waves so violent
they felt inhuman.

It wasn't just pain.
It was invasion.
A fire that lived beneath my skin, consuming me
from the inside out.

Every nerve screamed.
Every breath felt like betrayal.
My body—once strong, agile, athletic—
had become a burning cage I couldn't escape.

The heat was unbearable.
It didn't feel like a fever.
It felt like I was being punished by my own cells.

And still, my body wasn't whole.

My legs, my lower body,
felt like they'd floated away.
Weightless. Hollow. Gone.
I couldn't feel them.
And worse... I couldn't reach them.

They didn't feel like mine anymore.

At times, it even felt like they were hovering
somewhere above me—my legs, my butt,
all suspended midair—and in desperation,
I begged my parents, "Please... put them down."
But they were already down.
It was just my mind that couldn't find them.

My hands—my fingers—
a terrible feeling haunted me:
Like my fingers were glued together.
As if a thin, invisible membrane stretched
between them, webbed like a duck's foot.

It wasn't pain.
It was wrongness.
Unnatural. Disturbing.

I begged my parents:
"Please... separate them.
Please. It feels like they're stuck together.
It's driving me crazy."

They tried.
Gently.
Lovingly.
But there was nothing to fix.
Because the truth is:
My body no longer answered to me.

But the hardest battles didn't come during the day.
They came when the lights went out.

At night, without my parents by my side—
without stronger medication to hold back the storm—
I was left alone in the dark with the pain.

Hour after hour, it devoured me.
Like something alive, gnawing its way through my ribs.

Then, in the depths of that night,
when I cried out—sobbing, pleading for help—
a nurse appeared.

Not soft.
Not kind.

She leaned over me, looked straight
into my fear-soaked eyes, and hissed:

"Shut up."

Two words.
Two bullets.

They cut through the heat, the pain, the medication.
They told me that not everyone would meet
my suffering with mercy.
That sometimes, even in your most broken moment,
the world could be cruel.
Worse still, it could be indifferent.

In that moment—more than the diagnosis,
more than the paralysis—I felt abandoned.

But even as my body betrayed me,
even as my soul fractured under the weight of pain
and loneliness—an ember waited, hidden but alive.

A flicker.
A whisper.
A glimmer.

No.

I didn't know how.
I didn't know when.
But I made a promise to myself:

This will not be the end of me.

A Room of Our Own

As the first brutal week in the hospital crawled
to an end, I was moved from the intensive care unit
into a regular hospital room.
On paper, it was a step forward.
In reality, it felt like falling into a deeper
kind of loneliness. Despite my fragile state,
the hospital's rules remained firm:
no parents allowed to stay overnight.
Each evening, after the nurses made their rounds,
my mom and dad were forced to leave,
their tearful goodbyes hanging heavy in the air.

And each night, as the door clicked shut behind them,
fear settled in like an unwelcome guest.
Alone in the darkness, I listened
to the metronome of devices,
the distant shuffles of strangers in the halls,
the heavy silence pressing down on my chest.
I fought tears I was too exhausted to shed.
I fought the rising panic—
that maybe... this would be my life now.
But my mom was not one to accept defeat.

Fueled by something deeper than anger—
something raw, primal, and unbreakable—
she stormed into the hospital director's office,
a mother bear cloaked in contained fire.
With a voice fluttering with fury and love,
she demanded a simple truth:
No child should have to suffer alone.
Her words, spoken from the untamed
corners of her heart, broke through the walls
bureaucracy had built.

And so, against hospital policy,
a new sanctuary was created.
A narrow room—barely big enough for two beds,
its walls scuffed, its window fractured with age.
Our small refuge against the storm.

For the next five months, my mom never left my side.
By day, she was my advocate, my nurse, my voice.
By night, she was the hand I reached for in the dark,
the lullaby that soothed the terror in my chest,
the living proof that even in the bleakest places,
love could build a home.

We laughed sometimes, despite everything.
We cried often.
We survived together.

And that little hospital room, with its chipped paint
and the steady rhythm of life around us,
became more than just four walls.
It became a promise:
You are not alone.
You will never be alone.

The Walls That Held Me

Days collapsed into each other
inside that cramped hospital room.
Morning and night lost their meaning.
Time became a slow, endless river,
carrying me further away from the life I once knew.
I spent most hours staring up at the ceiling,
its pale, timeworn surface the only thing
unchanged in a world that kept shifting beneath me.
The soft shuffle of nurses' footsteps,
the occasional murmur of doctors outside the door—
these became the background music
of my new existence.

Even in that heavy grayness, small traces of grace
found their way in.

Friends and family poured their love into the room,
sending colorful cards, hand-drawn pictures,
and letters filled with prayers and promises.
Bright banners taped to the walls
whispered words of encouragement,
transforming the hospital space into a harbor
mended by compassion.

Each message was a thread
pulling me back from despair,
each signature a hand reaching out to lift me up.
I clung to the idea that maybe this was just temporary.
That someday soon, I would hold my racquet again,
feel the court beneath my shoes, chase my dreams
across a sunlit net.

But hope, as I was learning, is fleeting.
One afternoon, a new doctor entered our room—
one I hadn't seen before.
Without warning, without softness, he delivered
his verdict like a blow to the chest.
"You may never move again," he said flatly.
"You may not even be able to sit in a wheelchair."

The words sucked the air from the room.
The ceiling above me swam.
My dreams—so delicately woven back together—
were torn apart in a single, brutal moment.
I was shattered, suspended in shock,
unable to absorb the full weight of it.

And before I could even begin to process
the devastation, my mom was already on her feet.
I watched her, struck, as she stood with a ferocity
I had never seen before—small in stature
but towering in spirit.
She marched across the room
and, with a voice as sharp as broken glass,
she pointed to the door. "Get out," she commanded.
There was no hesitation.
No second chances.

The doctor faltered,
mumbled something under his breath,
and disappeared down the hall,
leaving behind a silence thick with anger,
heartbreak, and something burning still:

Love.

My mom sat beside me, her hand finding mine,
still shaking from the confrontation.

"You don't listen to him," she said firmly,
"You are going to fight.
You are going to heal.
And you are going to live."

That moment, I understood something
words could never fully explain:
Love doesn't just comfort.
Sometimes, it fights.
Sometimes, it becomes the shield that protects
your dreams when you are too broken
to protect them yourself.

I felt it—the shy flame of hope shining back
to life inside me.

A Christmas Like No Other

As December deepened and the world outside
blanketed itself in winter's hush,
our room transformed, like a small miracle.

Despite the wires and beeping monitors,
despite the weight of uncertainty pressing
down on us, the air filled with magic.
The nurses—those everyday angels—
wrapped the bare walls in warmth and laughter,
stringing twinkling lights across windows
and pinning handmade decorations above my bed.
They became more than caretakers.
They became friends.
Their kindness swaddled itself around me
like a soft quilt—gentle touches, whispered jokes,
small moments of human connection
that reminded me life was still beautiful, even here.

And then, as Christmas neared,
an unexpected light shone even brighter.
A family—the Kuchařovi,
beautiful in their generosity and spirit—
reached out to us.
They brought not just gifts,
but a sense of belonging, a reminder
that we were not forgotten, not alone.
They arrived with armfuls of warmth—food,
decorations, and most precious of all:
a Christmas tree.

The tree stood in the corner of the room,
its branches heavy with ornaments,
tiny lights blinking like a constellation of hope.
Under its glow, the hospital walls seemed to fade away,
and for the first time in weeks,
it truly felt like Christmas.

Beneath the shimmer of colored lights,
my heart longed to give back.

Confined to my bed, unable to shop
or wrap presents with my own hands,
I turned to a kind-hearted nurse,
entrusting her with a secret mission:
to find a small gift for my parents,
something simple, something that could never
measure up to their sacrifices,
but might at least offer,
"Thank you. I see you. I love you."

The gifts we chose were humble.
But the love behind them was endless.
It wasn't grand gestures that defined love.
It was the stubborn persistence of showing up.
It was the willingness to stay,
to fight, to hope—together.

As for my own Christmas wishes,
they remained achingly simple.

I wished for my legs and arms to move.
I wished to hold a racquet again.
I wished for a CD player to fill the long,
heavy nights with music and memories,
to drown out the sound of hospital instruments
with songs that once made me feel alive.

But even without those things, that Christmas
gave me a gift no one could ever take away:
the unshakable truth that love—
raw, imperfect, fierce—
was the greatest healing force of all.

Windows to the World

Inside our pocket-sized hospital room, time seemed
to stand still. The furniture, the scuffed walls,
even the faded linoleum floors—
nothing ever changed. Day after day,
it was the same view, the same medical hum,
the same heavy stillness pressing against the windows.

There was only one window in the room,
small and square, perched just high enough
to offer a glimpse of the outside world. From it,
my mom could see the hospital's helicopter pad—
where life and death collided
in moments of flashing urgency. Where helicopters,
heavy with hope or grief, came and went
with the roar of engines and the whir of blades.

But my bed faced the opposite wall.
I couldn't see it. I couldn't even turn my head
to catch a trace of movement my mom described.
The world, for me, remained a hollow box.
Yet my mom refused to let me feel left behind.

Each time a helicopter landed, she would lean close
and paint it for me with her words.
Through her, the helicopters became
more than distant sounds.
They became living stories that anchored me
to the world still spinning outside my hospital walls.
As she spoke, I closed my eyes and saw it all.
I saw the bright colors streak across the sky.
I heard the thunder of the engines in my chest.
I felt, for a moment, weightless again—
free, moving, alive.

My mom's words poured color back into a life
that had turned unbearably gray.
Through her eyes, I could still belong to a world
I could no longer touch.

Even in the absence of everything familiar,
it's not strength that carries us—it's connection.
It's knowing someone still believes you can fly.

The First Fragile Victories

As the new year arrived, time inside the hospital
fell into a slow, painful rhythm.
The walls stayed the same.
The beeping threaded through the hours.
But inside my broken body,
a silent battle had begun.
Rehabilitation was no miracle cure.
It was a painstaking war fought in inches, not miles.
A war between mind and muscle.
A war between hope and despair.

Every day, I strained with everything I had
just to will a single finger to move.
Sometimes I squeezed a nurse's hand
with the faintest twitch, feeling like
I was pulling myself back from the edge of a cliff.
Other times, I fought for hours without even
the smallest reward, frustration gnawing at me.

Learning to write again felt like
trying to teach a river to flow backward.
The severed connection between thought and action
left my hands clumsy, not my own.
But I refused to surrender.

The therapists placed a soft foam ball into my palm
and pushed a pencil through it—
creating a makeshift tool that gave me just
enough stability to try.
Letter by painful letter, I fought to remember
how to speak through my hands.
Some days the pencil slid uselessly across the paper.
Some days I broke down in tears of frustration,
unable to recognize the shaky lines
I managed to scrawl. But I kept trying.
And then, one afternoon, it happened.

Through the imperfect effort of my fingers,
words began to take shape:
I love you, Mom and Dad.

The sentence sprawled crookedly across the page,
barely legible—but it was there.
It was real.

Tears blurred my vision as my mom
clutched the paper to her chest,
her face softening into pure, unguarded emotion.
With that, we weren't patients
and caretakers anymore.
We were just a family, connected together
by a love that even fate couldn't tear apart.

But the journey had only begun.
Tasks that once felt effortless—
feeding myself, lifting a spoon—
now towered like cliffs before me.
The simple motion of hand to mouth
became a hard-won dance of balance,
strength, and the will to go on.

How do you re-learn something
your body used to do without thinking?
How do you command hands
that no longer seem to belong to you?
Each faltering attempt was a lesson in patience.
Each shaky lift of the spoon
was the shape courage took.
Some days the spoon spilled halfway up.
Some days I couldn't even grasp it at all.
And then I realized:
This is where your real strength begins.

And so, day by day,
I rewrote the limits the world tried to place on me,
redefining what was possible,
daring to believe that even shattered dreams
could be rebuilt, stronger than before.

The First Ascent

Rehabilitation moved with its own relentless rhythm.
Slow. Steady. Merciless.

Each day bled into the next, bound together
by a thousand small battles fought inside the walls
of that tiny hospital room.
Hidden inside that exhaustion, resilience
was being born.
Then came the day I had both longed for and feared.
It was time to rise.
Not walk. Not run.
Just sit. Just stand.
Simple words, but monumental climbs
for a body that had forgotten how to obey.

A team of therapists and nurses gathered around me,
their faces patient but serious.
They spoke gently, explaining the plan:
the bed would tilt upward,
straps across my chest and legs would hold me safely,
and they would guide me through the first
delicate moments of vertical life.

My heart hammered against my ribs.
Fear clamped its hands around my throat.

What if I fainted?
What if the blood rushed out of my head
and left me crumpled on the floor?
What if my body, so foreign and unpredictable now,
betrayed me once again?

I closed my eyes as they began.
The bed's slow hum filled the room,
lifting me inch by inch
out of the world I had known—
the world of lying flat, of ceilings and stillness—
and into the terrifying unknown of movement,
weight, gravity.
My legs dangled uselessly.
My head spun.
Every nerve screamed in confusion.
But somehow—somehow—I stayed upright.

Held by straps, held by hands, held by faith.
It wasn't graceful.
It wasn't triumphant.
It was shaky, awkward, and overwhelming.
But it was standing.
As the blood surged painfully back through
my veins, and the world came back into focus around
me, a tear slipped down my cheek.
Not for what I had lost.
But for what I was beginning to find again:
A way forward.
A way back to myself.
One unsteady step at a time.

The Smallest Miracles

Even as light slowly began to stir beneath the surface,
I remained still—completely, utterly still.
My body, once a vessel of strength and motion,
now lay quiet, frail, tethered by IV lines
and surrounded by monitors that hummed
on my behalf. I couldn't sit. I couldn't lift my head.
I couldn't move or gesture
or ask the world to look more closely
at what I was beginning to feel inside.
Every shift in position had to be done for me,
every sensation filtered through a fog I couldn't
push through. But even in that pause,
I listened—listened with a different kind of awareness,
a sacred calm that tuned me
in to the faintest whispers of life.
And then, one day, stillness cracked open.
A strange sensation bloomed in my foot—
so slight it could have been imagined.
But it wasn't.

My toe... moved.

Just a pulse.
A flicker.
An echo from a place long silent.
I couldn't see it.
I couldn't point to it.
But I felt it. I knew it.

And from the depths of my paralyzed body,
a force surged—hope, raw and electric.
I called out with the only thing I had—my voice.
Soft, frayed, but sure.

"Mom... my toe moved."

My mom rushed to my side,
eyes searching, heart wide open.
Without hesitation, she crouched low
at the end of the bed, tears already rising
before she even saw it.
She waited, holding her breath.
And there it was—again.
The smallest twitch.
But it was real.
Her hands flew to her face.
She didn't speak.
She didn't have to.
That night, the air in the room felt different—
lighter, fuller, sacred.
It wasn't a miracle the doctors could chart or explain.
But to us, it was everything.

It was the moment we knew that healing had begun—
not just in body, but in spirit.
From that day forward, I began to squeeze my toes—
not because I could feel them,
but because I believed in them.
I believed in what was possible.
I believed in myself, even when my body
refused to answer.
And every time I tried—again and again,
in silence, in stillness, without anyone watching—
my mom would sit with me, her hand resting gently
on my arm, lending me her strength without a word.
She knew. She always knew.
These were not just movements.
They were declarations.
I am still here.
I am still fighting.
And I will find my way back.

The Mirror and the Sky

The helicopters had always been just out of reach.
One afternoon, after countless failed attempts
to help me see them landing, my mom
reached for a small, unadorned mirror—
just big enough to fit in her palm. With hope,
she began tilting it again, adjusting its angle
in every direction.

Left. Right. Higher. Lower.
Her hands moved through the air like a musician
searching for the perfect note.

Still—nothing.
Only fragments of ceiling,
the glare of fluorescent lights, and the faded curtain
near the window. The disappointment, by now,
was familiar—quiet, shared, and heavy.

And then...
Out of nowhere, from a place deeper
than frustration, deeper than longing,
I felt it rise inside me—urgent, unmistakable.

"No, over there!" I said, my voice cutting through
the tension like a beam of light.
And then—my arm lifted.
All on its own.
Without help.
Without hesitation.
I pointed.
Clearly.
Purposefully.
It wasn't just a reflex. It was power. It was choice.
I had never done that before—not since the accident.
She followed the direction of my raised arm.
Adjusted the mirror one final time, and there it was.

The helicopter.

Spinning.
Gleaming.
Landing.

I saw it.

As my heart swelled with disbelief,
a fear rushed in.
Fear that I might forget how I'd done it.
That this miracle might fade
as quickly as it came.
So I did the only thing I could.
I lifted my arm again.
And again.
And again.
I raised it over and over,
branding the motion into my body,
to keep the memory alive, to tell my nervous system:
"Remember this. Don't let it go."
That day, the helicopter wasn't
the only thing that landed. Hope did too.
From that moment on, my arm was no longer still.
It was a promise.
A doorway opening back to myself.

The Silence of Touch

Even as my body began to obey again—lifting an arm,
curling a toe, inching toward recovery,
there was something missing.
Something I couldn't force or fake or will into being.
I couldn't feel.
No matter how many milestones I reached,
the world remained strangely distant,
as though I were wrapped in invisible gauze.
Nurses pinched my skin.
Doctors pressed instruments against my legs.
But I felt nothing.
Not pain.
Not pressure.
Not presence.

It was as if I were floating just above myself—
watching, responding, even celebrating,
but never truly inhabiting my body.
There was motion. But no touch.
A ghost-like existence that separated me
from the very thing I was trying to return to.

Sometimes I stared at my own hands,
moving slowly, obediently but empty.
They were mine, and yet... they weren't.
No warmth. No texture.
No trace of what touch used to mean.
That emptiness became its own kind of ache.
Not sharp. Not searing. But vast.
And still, I pressed on.
Because even in the absence of sensation,
there was a presence of will.
A persistent belief that one day,
the silence would lift.
That one day, I would feel it all again.
But for now, I moved through a world I couldn't touch
and trusted that somehow... it would touch me back.

Wheels Beneath Me

Once I could stand without fainting,
once the risk of blood clots had passed,
a new phase of recovery began.
And with it came something
I had dreaded from the beginning.

The wheelchair.

It arrived one morning—navy blue, cold, and massive.
The wheels looked too large,
the metal too unforgiving.
It wasn't just a tool, it was a symbol.
A declaration to the world:

She can't walk.

The sight of it made my stomach clench.
Shame.
Embarrassment.
Loss.
I hated it instantly.

My body recoiled. My spirit flared.
No one had asked me if I was ready.
No one had asked if I wanted it.
They simply wheeled it in, as if it belonged to me.
I wanted to scream.
I wasn't that girl.
I wasn't this.
But the nurses and doctors were firm.

It wasn't a punishment—it was progress.
A step forward.
A way out of the room that had held me for so long.
And so, with a heart heavy with resistance,
I was lifted into the chair.
I said nothing.
But inside, I burned.

Being wheeled down the hall for the first time
felt like being paraded.
My limbs, still slow and uncertain,
rested awkwardly in place.
My eyes darted, avoiding contact.
I didn't want pity.
I didn't want stares.

But then, there they were.
As we turned the corner of the long corridor,
I saw them.

Other children.

Some younger, some older.
Some held in casts, some with shaved heads
and IV poles. Others in wheelchairs just like mine.
And they weren't ashamed. They smiled. They waved.
Some rolled past with confident ease,
chatting with nurses like old friends.
They weren't defined by the chairs beneath them.
They were alive—fighting, surviving, moving forward.

A part of me let go.
There, among them, I felt seen—not as broken,
but as someone who belonged
to a hidden army of fighters.
Still, even as that first thread of belonging
flowed through me, I made a vow to myself:
This will not be where I stay.
I would use the chair.
I would respect the journey.
But I would not surrender to it.

With every rotation of those wheels,
I carried the fire of that promise—
that one day, I would stand again.
Walk again.
Leave the chair behind—
not from shame
or maybe just a little
but from faith that I was meant to move.
And that belief, even on the hardest days,
never let go of me.

The Boy, the Gum,
and the Freedom of Laughter

When I moved from the quiet cocoon of neurosurgery
to the wider world of the neurology wing,
the world began to stretch open in ways
I hadn't imagined.
The walls didn't feel quite as close.
The hallways seemed to breathe again,
the days a little lighter.
There was space now—not just for progress,
but for people. For connection.

That's when I met him.

A boy with an easy smile and a spark in his eyes,
full of mischief and life.
He rolled through the halls
like they were his playground,
unbothered by the weight of diagnoses.
To me, he became a kindred spirit.
Someone who saw past the monitors and medicine
and found reasons to laugh in the in-between.

One afternoon, with a grin full of promise,
he proposed an adventure:
"Wanna take the wheelchair out for a spin?"

My mom wasn't entirely thrilled with his idea—
afraid he might flip me out of my wheelchair.
But she also believed it might be good for my spirit.

And so just like that, we were off.

Rolling through the hospital like renegades,
dodging nurses and rules, pretending
we had somewhere far more important to be.
The wind didn't blow in our hair,
but it did in our hearts. In those moments,
the wheelchair wasn't a prison.
It was freedom. It was flight.

And then, his next idea sparked.
"Movie night. Common room. You in?"

I nodded, trying to play it cool, even as my heart
thudded louder than the hospital clocks.

As we sat side by side, watching the screen,
a wild thought crossed my mind.
What if he tries to kiss me?

In an instant, I froze.
I was chewing gum.

A crisis.

Where would I put it if that moment came?
I couldn't exactly get up and throw it away.
So my mind raced:
Stick it in my hair? No.
Tuck it under the wheelchair seat? Gross.
Smear it on my T-shirt? Absolutely not.

Then, with the logic of a girl half-terrified
and half-hoping, I slipped it into the safest place
I could think of—my pocket.

He didn't kiss me.

But hours later, I discovered the gum had melted
into a sticky disaster, gluing itself
to the fabric like a little pink badge
of my over-prepared imagination.
We laughed about it. Hard.

It wasn't just about gum.
Or kisses.
Or even freedom.

It was about being a teenager again.
Even here. Even now.

In those late-night rides and shared jokes,
I found pieces of myself returning—
the parts that loved connection, flirted with adventure,
and saw the humor in the mess.

The hospital was still a place of pain.
But in the company of this boy, and the friendships
that blossomed between drips and dreams,
it also became a place where life continued.
Where laughter still lived.
Where resilience could look like joy, too.

The Dance Before the Steps

As the long road of rehabilitation reached
a critical turning point, the challenge
lay before me—learning to walk again.

The very idea felt surreal.
My legs, still paralyzed and heavy.
There was no sensation. No feedback.
Just vain weight—limbs drifting at the edge
of awareness, distant and strange.

The rhythm of walking—once so instinctive,
so blended into my childhood—had vanished.
What had once been second nature
now felt like a forgotten language.
One foot, then the other?
It no longer made sense.

Fear gripped me tighter than gravity.
The thought of falling, of losing control,
of nose-diving toward the floor without the strength
to catch myself. It haunted me.
Then—gentle as breath—came a memory.

A dance.

My mom and me, years ago, twirling clumsily
through our living room, my tiny feet placed
on top of hers. She would take a step,
and I would go with her—held upright by her arms.
We called it the "drunk bear dance"—
a swirl of laughter, uncoordinated steps,
and the kind of closeness that never really left me.

My mom smiled and said, "Let's try our dance."

She placed my feet gently on top of hers again.
Her arms hugged around me.
And began to move.
Slowly.
One step.
Then another.

With every shift of her weight, my body followed.
Held, supported, safe.
It wasn't walking. Not yet.
But it reminded me what it felt like to move forward.

Then she looked at me and said:
"Let's try to walk—with support."

The nurses moved in—four of them,
gentle and strong, forming a protective circle
around me. Their hands steadied my frame,
guiding my legs, holding me from every angle.

And with my mom in front of me—we stepped.

Not far.
Not freely.
But forward.

My legs were limp, my body hesitant.
I couldn't feel the ground beneath me.
But I moved.
We moved.

And in that tremulous motion carried by others,
I took my first step toward becoming whole again.

The First Shower

It came without ceremony.
A moment so simple it might've gone unnoticed
by the world—but to me, it was everything.

A shower.

Months had passed since I last felt the warmth
of water on my skin. What once was a daily routine
now loomed before me like a wave.
Unfamiliar, intimidating, and laced with fear.

This wasn't just about hygiene.
It was about facing the unknown.
Because in my mind, water was no longer gentle.
It had become something sharp and punishing.

I imagined a thousand needles falling
from the shower head. Each droplet a tiny spear
ready to strike. The thought alone made me shiver.
My skin, already distant to me,
felt too disconnected to endure it. I was terrified.

But my mom was brave for both of us.

With her hands and her voice, she guided me
toward the threshold.

Each small movement felt enormous.
The tile beneath my feet, the cool air on my skin,
the sound of water beginning to fall.
It all pressed against the edges of my courage.

Then, slowly, I stepped in.

I braced myself for pain. For shock.
For the betrayal of sensation I no longer trusted.

But it didn't come.

Instead, the water met me with kindness.

Warm. Gentle. Forgiving.

It slid across my shoulders like silk.
It trickled down my back and arms like memory.
And all at once, the fear melted.

There were no needles. No pain. Just relief.

I closed my eyes.
And I breathed.

In that stream of water, I felt something wash over me
that I hadn't known I needed—
belonging.

To my body.
To life.
To the part of me still capable of joy.

My mom stood close, letting me feel
the moment fully.

We didn't speak.
But we both knew.

This wasn't just a shower.
It was a return.
A baptism of bravery.
A gentle assertion that I was still here,
still healing, still human.

I remembered what it felt like to be alive.

A Touch Beyond Touch

It was just another night.
It held something tender.
Something unspoken passed
between my mom and me.

It was a moment held not with sound,
but with presence. Not with answers,
but with something far more sacred: mystery.

The hospital room was dim, cloaked in shadow.
I couldn't see her from where I lay.
And I couldn't feel her—not with my body.
My skin had long forgotten touch.

The weight of endless days had begun
to take its toll on her.
For weeks she had been my anchor, my fire,
the voice of assurance when I had none.
But that night, the light she carried for both of us
faltered.

She turned away, pressing a pillow to her face,
trying to muffle the sound of her breaking heart.
The silence between us wasn't empty.
It was full of everything she didn't want me to hear.

Needing comfort she couldn't find,
she placed her hands on her belly
and began to rub slow, absent circles.
An unconscious gesture, a self-soothing rhythm,
an aching mom trying not to fall apart.

And then... it happened.

I felt it.

Not on my skin.
Not through restored nerves.
But in the space where spirit meets instinct.

I felt a hand moving gently across my belly.
Soft.
Rhythmic.
Familiar.

Startled, I whispered:

"Mom... are you touching my belly?"

She turned to me.

Time stopped.

Her tears did not.

For a moment, she just stared—
words lost between disbelief and awe.

Because she hadn't touched me.
She had only touched herself.
And yet, somehow... I knew.

In that glance, the storm inside her cleared.
Not despair this time, but light.

All the doubt she had carried—every muted fear,
every lingering what if—evaporated.

She had been teetering at the edge of losing hope.
And now, because of that single question,
she believed again.

Not because a doctor told her to.
Not because the charts looked better.
But because something real had passed between us.
Something science couldn't name.
Something only a mom could understand.

Maybe it was a miracle.
Maybe it was grace.
Maybe it was simply love.
Moving freely between us, unhindered by paralysis,
untouched by logic.

But from that night on, her belief in my recovery
no longer wavered.

We both knew:
I was coming back.
And she would be there—every single step of the way.

The Fifth Month

As the fifth month in the hospital approached,
the walls that once felt cold and unfamiliar
begun to feel like—

a home.
A battleground.
A sanctuary.

Day by day, my body had slowly responded
to the unceasing symphony of therapies—
each one its own kind of breakthrough.
Massages that coaxed life back into stiff limbs.
Reflexology that awakened nerves long silent.
Heavy machinery that taught my legs
how to bear weight again.
Ergotherapy that helped me relearn the simplest
motions of independence.

Each tool, each technique, each act of care
had become a thread in the fabric of my healing.

But healing, I was learning, doesn't stand still.
It asks for more.

And so, the time had come to say goodbye.

Goodbye to the nurses who had become
my second family—those who had held my hand
in pain, cheered my smallest victories,
and made me feel safe when my body no longer did.

Goodbye to the doctors who had saved my life.

Gratitude filled every breath.
And so did sorrow.

Because it's not easy to leave the place
where you first began to rise again.

But healing has many homes.

And mine was about to move.

With a heart weighted by farewell,
and a spirit shaped by everything I had endured,
I prepared to take the next step.

This time toward a children's spa for rehabilitation.
A new chapter of recovery created specifically
for kids like me.

There, I was told, I'd find specialized care.
More therapy.
More time.
More hope.

But also... uncertainty.
New faces. New fears.
A new place to grow.

And as the hospital doors closed behind me,
I knew I wasn't just leaving a room or the corridors.

I was leaving the girl who had arrived five months ago.

The one who didn't yet know she could fight.
The one who didn't yet believe she could rise.

In her place, a new version of me emerged.
Still healing, still searching,
but no longer afraid to begin again.

The Weight of the First Steps

Leaning forward with a tentative mixture of fear
and determination, I took my first steps
beyond the hospital—a girl rebuilt, but not yet whole.

Each step was wobbly, unsteady.
Each motion demanded more than it should have.
My right side still numb, the ground beneath my feet
dull and strange.
I moved like a visitor in my own body.

The world looked familiar.
But nothing felt the same.

Every sensation carried both promise and pain.
I had dreamed of walking again.
Now that I was, why did it feel so weirdly off?

The shadow of worry loomed larger than I expected.

Would this body ever feel like mine again?
Would I ever run, dance, or even walk freely
without wondering what might give out next?

Simple things—eating, dressing, standing—
had become questions rather than guarantees.
Would I ever feed myself again without fumbling?
Would I trust my hands to serve me, not betray me?

And beyond the body, deeper questions came.

Would I be loved in this new form?
Would someone ever hold me without flinching?
See beyond the wheelchair, beyond the struggle,
and into me?

Would friends stay?
Or drift away, unsure how to belong
to my new world?

Would I ever be able to have children?
Hold a baby in my arms?

These thoughts arrived like ghosts at night.
Silent, cold, and hard to banish.

But even in that darkness, a pulse of light held on.

A conviction, however small, that I wasn't done.
That healing doesn't always look like perfection.
That love isn't bound to what a body can do.

That miracles are quiet, and still unfolding.

So I kept walking.

Clumsy. Brave. Still afraid.
But walking toward something.
A life beyond fear.
A life where I could still be whole.

Epilogue

Some Miracles Begin in the Dark

In life's subtle architecture, every thread
is woven with intention.
Each event, each experience—no matter how joyful
or painful—reveals its purpose.
Nothing is random.
Even the hardest moments carry meaning.

When life shifts unexpectedly, when we face trials
we never saw coming, it's natural to ask why.
But perhaps the more powerful question is:
What is this here to teach me?
Who am I becoming because of it?

Understanding that *everything happens for a reason*
does not erase the pain—but it transforms it.
It invites us to see our circumstances
not as punishments, but as passageways.
Not endings, but beginnings.

You may not feel strong.
You may be walking through something so heavy,
so dark, it makes you forget who you are.
But let me remind you:
You are still becoming.
And the story is not over.

Every challenge you face is not here to destroy you.
It's here to awaken something greater in you.
Resilience. Compassion. Purpose.

Your wounds may one day become
someone else's lantern.

When we choose to rise, to learn, to share
what we've been through, we create a ripple—
one that reaches people we may never meet,
on days we'll never see, offering light exactly
when they need it most.

So if today feels heavy,
if you're standing at the edge of something painful
and you don't know how to move forward—hold on.

You are not alone.
You are not broken.
You are rising.

Walk this life with an open heart.
Let the hard moments shape you, not silence you.
Trust the journey, even when the map makes no sense.
And when in doubt, remember this:

Some of life's greatest miracles begin in the dark.
And so did mine.

Acknowledgments

To my parents—
There are no words wide enough or deep enough.
Thank you for holding my body
when it couldn't move, and holding my heart
when it almost gave up.
You never let me fall completely.
This book is yours as much as it is mine.

To my younger self—
You were braver than you knew.
Even in the silence, even in the fire,
you were blooming into who you were always
meant to be.

To the friends—
from childhood, from tennis, from life—who stayed—
Your letters, your drawings, your photos...
they were more than just paper. They were light.
You reminded me that I wasn't forgotten.
That I still had a place in this world,
even from a hospital bed.
Thank you for seeing me when I couldn't see myself.
For staying close when so many disappeared.
I will never forget the way
your words carried me through.

To every doctor, nurse, therapist, and soul
who helped me find my way back—thank you.
Thank you for treating me not just as a patient,
but as a person.
For moving swiftly when time was slipping,
for honoring my voice when so much
felt out of my control,
and for holding the pieces of my body and spirit
with quiet strength.
You may never know the impact of those moments—
but I will never forget them.

And to one doctor in particular—
Dr. Miloslav Holub—
thank you for saving not only my life,
but for caring for me with unwavering dedication
from the beginning to this very day.
Your wisdom, calm, and compassion
have carried me through more than I can name.
You are a gift I will always cherish.

To the readers who open this book with tenderness—
you are why I wrote this.

To the unseen hands of grace,
the whispers of the soul, and the healing that came
when I finally said yes to telling the truth—thank you.

And to my family today—
my husband, whose strength holds more
than words ever could,
and my beautiful sons,
who remind me each day that joy
is never lost to the past,
but recreated in every moment we choose love.

You helped me come home to myself.

Letters, Memories, and Love

These pages hold just a few of the many moments
that live in my heart.
Some memories I carry like stones in my pocket,
others like stardust in the sky.
Just because a moment isn't here
doesn't mean it isn't loved.

To everyone who walked beside me,
in silence or in story—
thank you.

Já si pamatuju ze školních let s tebou,
kdy jsme po vyučování šly někdy k vám domů.
A tuším, že jsme začaly polštářovou bitvu—
a já trefila křišťálový lustr a rozbila ho.
A bály jsme se, co na to řeknou vaši,
až přijdou domů a uvidí to.

— Janička
Spolužačka z lavice i ze života

I remember those school days with you,
when sometimes after class we'd walk to your house.
One day, we started a pillow fight—
and I hit your crystal chandelier. It shattered.
We stood there frozen,
our laughter turning into silence,
wondering what your parents would say
when they walked in and saw it.

— Janička
Classmate in school—and in life

Vzpomínám, jak jsi nikdy nezkazila žádnou srandu
a měla jsi vždycky dobrou náladu.
Jak jsi do sebe ládovala obrovské bagety.
Jak jsi kvůli mně zůstala v horší skupině angličtinářů,
abych od tebe mohla opisovat.
Ráda taky vzpomínám na naše návštěvy obchoďáku.
Mám tě moc ráda, Lucíčku.

— Pája
Spolužačka z vysoké školy
Přítelkyně, která zůstala v mém srdci
Kamarádka se smíchem v očích

I remember how you never spoiled a single joke,
and how you were always in a good mood.
How you stuffed yourself with those giant baguettes.
How you stayed in the weaker English group
just for me, so I could copy your homework.
I also remember our trips to the shopping mall.
I love you so much, Lucíčku.

— Pája
University classmate
A friend who stayed in my heart
A girl with laughter in her eyes

138

With Lucka Hradecká –
Before the match. After the laughter.

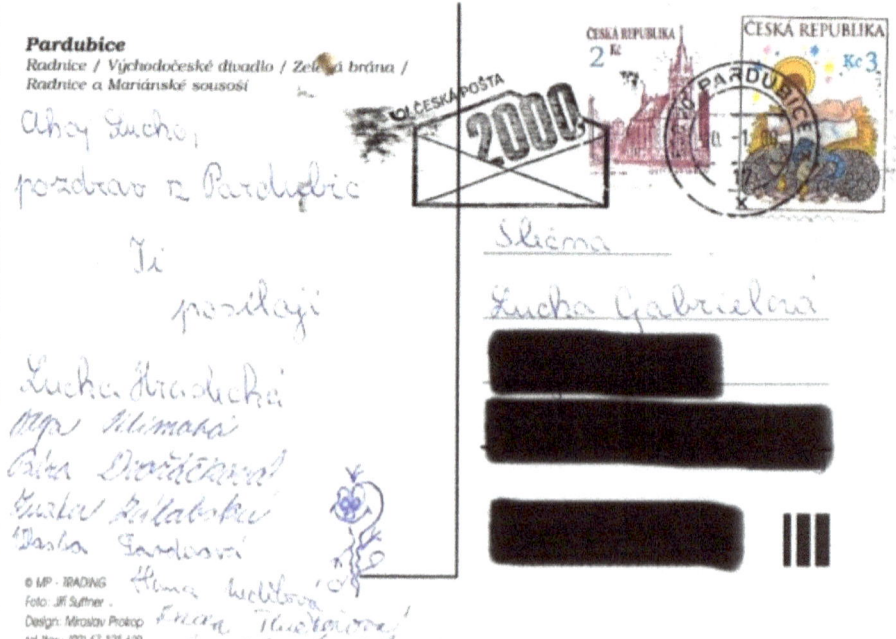

Pardubice
Radnice / Východočeské divadlo / Zelená brána /
Radnice a Mariánské sousoší

Ahoj Lucho,

pozdrav z Pardubic

Ti

posílají

Lucka Hradecká
Mgr. Ulimaná
Petra Dvořáčková
Gustav Bilabský
Dasha Santová

© MP - TRADING
Foto: Jiří Suttner
Design: Miroslav Prokop
tel./fax (02) 57 325 629

Slečna

Lucka Gabrielová

Katka Kočíbová and me –
More than a doubles team.
We shared tea, tournaments,
and too many laughs to count.

Čau Lucinko!

Jak se máš? Já s Kristou Horákovou docela dobře. Právě jsem u Kristy, kde teď sepisujeme pro Tebe dopis. Doufám, že se ti s Kdou a dědnou lépe. S Kristou, ale taky s celou rodinou na Tebe pořád myslíme. Víš, musíš se držet, abysme mohli zase spolu nahánět kluky a honit se za seniořky. Už se těším až přijdeš za náma na Moravu, kde zapaříme, ale to pořádně. Krista tady pořád blbě mluví, že neumí psát slohy nebo dopisy, ale snaží se. Doufám, že se začínáš zdokonalovat, třeba ve vylukování čísel na mobilu. Už se nemůžu s Kristou dočkat až konečně zavoláš. Budeme Ti moc držet pěsti, aby Ti to v nemocnici rychle utíkalo, ale věřím, že s maminkou Ti to půjde lépe. Už se nemůžu dočkat až se znovu setkáme.

Všichni Tě moc pozdravujou, takže:

Já, Krista, naše rodina, rodina Horáků, ale taky moji bráchové Pražák (Pavel) a Kája, ale určitě úplně všichni co Tě znají.

Tak Ahoj a opatruj se.
Hodně štěstí, zdraví a všechno co si přeješ.

142

Krista Horáková and me —
The clay still warm,
our smiles still real.

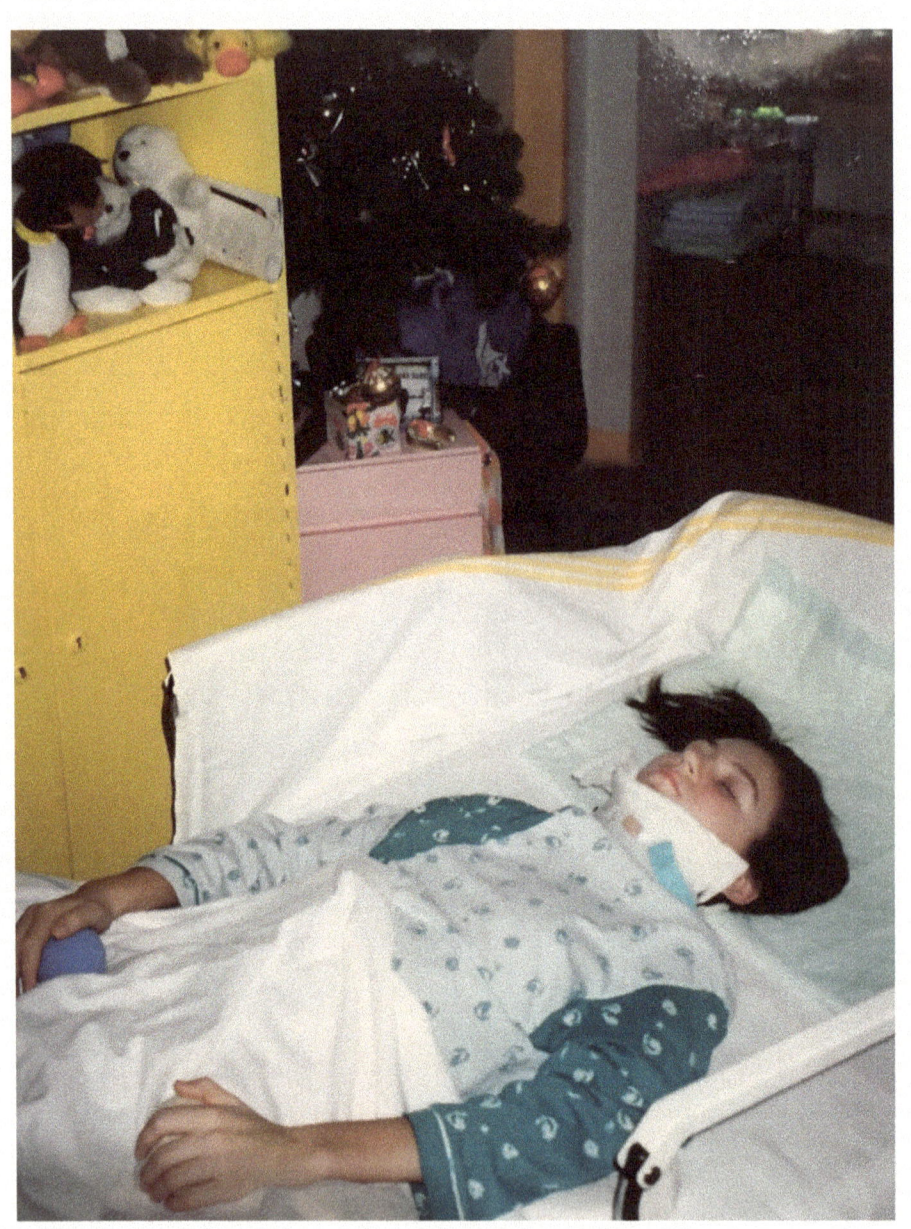

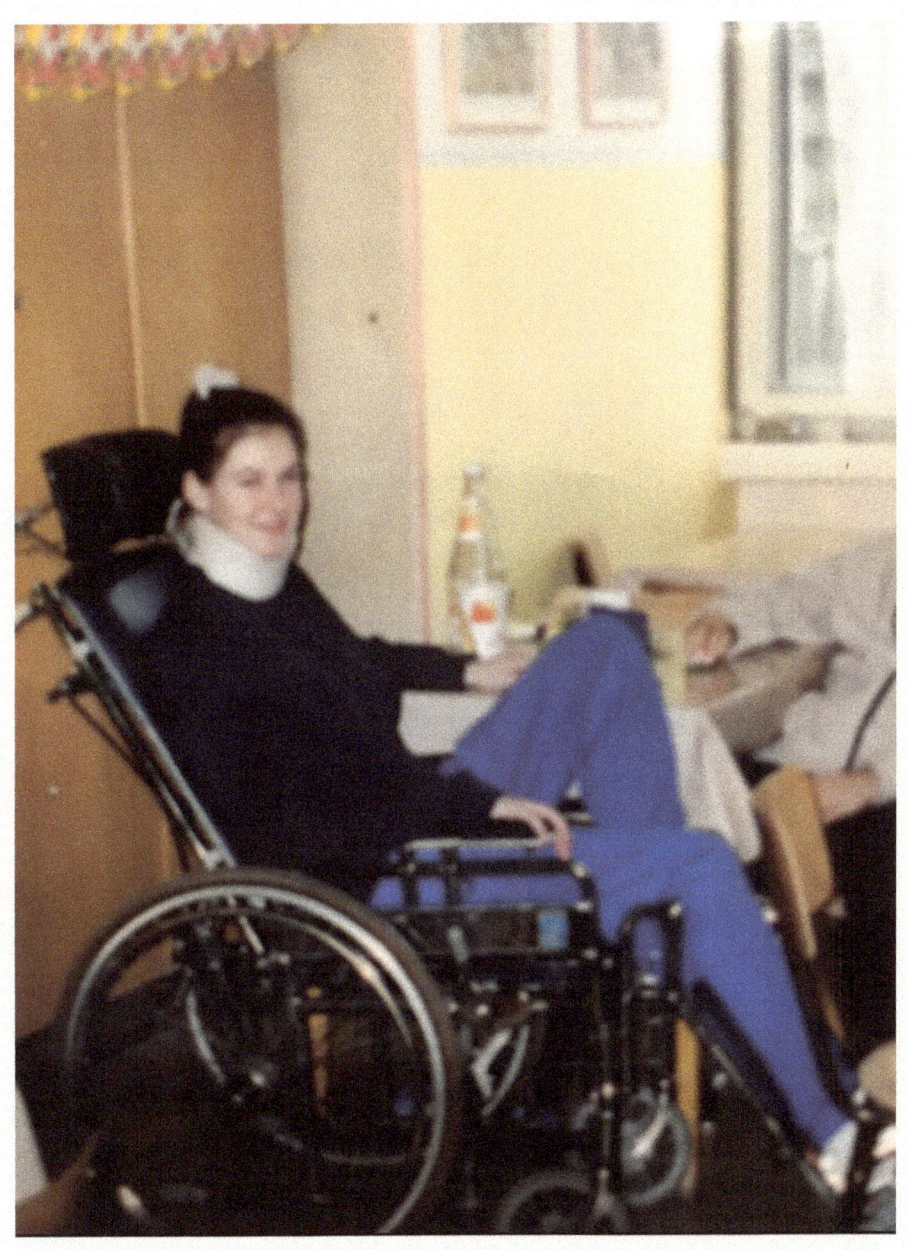

145

146

Maříková Klárka ... Terera Výkusová ... Bára
Katka Bílková Patrik Beutka Katka Šafránk

milá Lucko,

všichni Ti přejeme hodně zdraví, dobrou náladu,
trpělivost a pevnou vůli !
Těšíme se na Tebe !

Prázdn...

V Brně dne 6. 5. 2000

Pro Lucinku

Já nevím, co ty všechno víš,
ale přeji si, ať se brzy uzdravíš.

Dala jsem ti dáreček,
malý jak tvůj paleček.

Až uzdravíš se, budeme se smát,
až nasmějem se, půjdeme si hrát.

Když brzy ráno vstaneme,
tak se zase zasmějeme.

Smějeme se pořád,
v TV dávaj dobrej pořad.

TO VŠE OD TÉ
JEDNÉ HOLKY,
CELÝM JMÉNE
Veroniku!!!

DRAHÁ LUCKA! ŠŤASTNÉ PROŽITÍ VÁNOC, HODNĚ DÁRKŮ A JEŠTĚ VÍC TRPĚLIVOSTI DO NOVÉHO ROKU TI PŘEJÍ SESTŘIČKY Z NCHO-PA

23.12.99

...a při setkání se svými nejbližšími.

Praha, 4. února 2000

Ahoj, Lucko,

s velikým zájmem a nadějemi sledujeme Tvůj statečný boj o návrat do tenisového světa. Přejeme Ti, aby Tvá víra ani v nejmenším neutuchala a aby Tvá vůle následovala sportovce, kteří nad nepříznivým osudem dokázali zvítězit.

Přejeme Ti brzké uzdravení a rychlý návrat na tenisové kurty !!!

Ahoj Lucko!
Brzy se uzdrav.
Těším se na Tebe.
Ahoj Jana.

14. 12. 1999

Milá Lucinko!

Stále na Tebe myslíme
a držíme Ti palce
při uzdravování.
Až to půjde,
určitě Tě navštívíme.
Zatím bojuj, všichni
Ti přejí co nejrychlejší
zotavení!

Paulína Krajíčková
Michaela Krajíčková

151

About the Author

Lucie Gabrielová DeLaney is a writer, dreamer,
and former competitive tennis player whose journey
was forever changed by a spinal cord injury
at the age of fourteen. After years of silence, healing,
and rediscovery, she now shares her story
to inspire others walking through their own fires.

She believes that what breaks us can also awaken us
and that within every story of pain lives the potential
for purpose.

Lucie lives with her family,
creates with her whole heart,
and continues to remind others that no matter
what life brings...

This is not the end.

Connect with her on Instagram: @therealbravemia

www.ingramcontent.com/pod-product-compliance
Lightning Source LLC
Chambersburg PA
CBHW051623120626
46551CB00014B/1916